WELCOME
— to our —
WORLD

MOIRA BUTTERFIELD • HARRIET LYNAS

nosy crow

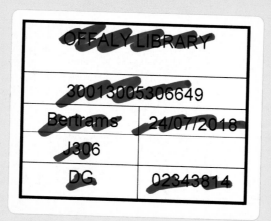

First published 2018 by Nosy Crow Ltd
The Crow's Nest, 14 Baden Place, Crosby Row
London, SE1 1YW

www.nosycrow.com

ISBN 978 1 78800 137 3

Nosy Crow and associated logos are trademarks
and/or registered trademarks of Nosy Crow Ltd.

A CIP catalogue record for this book is available from the British Library.

Printed in China.
Papers used by Nosy Crow are made from wood
grown in sustainable forests.

1 3 5 7 9 8 6 4 2

WELCOME
—to our—
WORLD

WRITTEN BY MOIRA BUTTERFIELD

Moira spent her childhood in lots of locations around Britain and Africa. She went on to study literature and become a children's author. She loves travelling and has almost succeeded in her ambition to visit every continent in the world (except for Antarctica, which sounds too chilly and slippery). Moira lives in Bath, Somerset, UK.

ILLUSTRATED BY HARRIET LYNAS

Harriet was born and raised in Korea. She loved doodling and decided to become an illustrator at the age of ten. She made that dream come true and now illustrates children's books, living in Hertfordshire, UK, with her husband and their son. When she is not drawing, she enjoys cooking exotic foods and country walking.

ALBANIA **AUSTRALIA** **BALI** **BANGLADESH** **BHUTAN** **BOLIVIA** **BOTSWANA** **BRAZIL**

CONTENTS

FRANCE **GREECE** **ICELAND** **ISRAEL** **LATVIA** **MALAWI** **MEXICO** **MOROCCO**

CAMBODIA

CANADA

COLOMBIA

COSTA RICA

CZECH REPUBLIC

DOMINICAN REPUBLIC

EGYPT

FIJI

Every country in the world has its own flag. These are just some of them. For a complete list of all the countries featured in this book, see page 64.

NEPAL

PERU

ROMANIA

SOUTH AFRICA

SPAIN

THAILAND

TONGA

VIETNAM

INTRODUCTION

Who is different but the same?

We sometimes speak **DIFFERENT** languages but we **ALL** talk to each other.

We sometimes wear **DIFFERENT** clothes but we **ALL** get dressed.

We sometimes eat **DIFFERENT** food but we **ALL** eat.

There are nearly 200 countries on the planet and more than 7 billion people who speak over 7,000 different languages. This book is about just a few of the many different things that people say and do in some of those places – otherwise it would be thousands of pages long!

People don't do the same thing every day. One day they might eat a hamburger and the next day they might eat a traditional dish from their country. One day somebody might put on jeans and a T-shirt and the next day they might wear a traditional costume for a festival or celebration. This book shares some of these special moments, but there are many more to discover.

Everyone loves to have fun, wherever they live. If you are very lucky, you will make friends from around the world and learn all about what they say and do, and how they are different to – and also the same as – you.

WELCOME TO OUR WORLD!

Some words might look difficult to say in English so you can use the pronunciation guides. These are just written guides. The best way to find out how to say words is to hear them spoken by a native speaker. You can also look up how to pronounce words on the internet.

HELLO...

Ways to greet friends

Wave hello to someone in a new way.
Which language do you
like the sound of?

Mongolian
SAIN UU
san-oh

Greek
GIASOU
yah-soo

Thai
SĂ WÀT DII
sa-wa-dee

Icelandic
HALLÓ
hal-oh

Nepalese
NAMASTE
nam-a-stay

Quechua
NAPAYKULLAYKI
nah-pie-coo-yah-key
(spoken in the Peruvian Andes)

8

MY NAME IS...

Names in different countries

Names aren't the same everywhere. Here's how to say "My name is" in different countries for a boy and a girl.

My name is...
EMMA
Canadian

Ég heiti...
(yey hey-tay)
GUNNAR
Icelandic

Ég heiti...
(yey hey-tay)
KRISTIN
Icelandic

A nevem...
ESZTER
Hungarian

My name is...
LIAM
Canadian

Zovem se...
AMAR
Bosnian

Watashi no namae wa
(watashi no na-my-wa)
YUI desu (des)
Japanese

Unë quhem...
(oon cue-hem)
ALBAN
Albanian

Em dic...
(um theek)
LUCAS
Catalan (from Andorra)

Zovem se...
ANIMA
Bosnian

Unë quhem...
(oon cue-hem)
ERSI
Albanian

Je m'appelle...
(zhuh mah-pell)
AWA
French (from Burkino Faso)

A nevem...
ADÁM
Hungarian

Watashi no namae wa
(watashi no na-my-wa)
HARUTO desu (des)
Japanese

Em dic...
(um theek)
LAIA
Catalan (from Andorra)

Je m'appelle...
(zhuh mah-pell)
BRAHIM
French (from Burkino Faso)

Meenya zavoot...
ANASTASIA
Russian

Mi nombre es...
(mee nom-bray es)
SANTIAGO
Venezuelan

Mi nombre es...
(mee nom-bray es)
ISABELLA
Venezuelan

Meenya zavoot...
ARTEM
Russian

GOOD MORNING, WORLD!

It's breakfast time

We all wake up and eat different breakfasts.
Which one of these international breakfast dishes would you like best?

Churros (*choo-ross*)
These sugary fried dough sticks
from Spain are often dipped in
chocolate sauce.

Miso soup (*mee-zo*)
In Japan, they eat a salty
savoury broth made with
soybean paste.

Syrniki (*sir-nicky*)
Sweet round pancakes made with
cottage cheese are eaten in
Russia and Ukraine.

Pho (*fu*)
A Vietnamese spicy noodle broth
made with chicken or beef.

Ackee and saltfish
Ackee is a type of fruit eaten in Jamaica.
It looks like scrambled egg when it's cooked.

What do you mostly eat for breakfast in the morning?

Congee (*con-jee*)
In China, people eat rice porridge mixed with meat, fish or vegetables.

Bread and butter with hagelslag (*har-gel-slarg*)
In Holland, people eat bread with chocolate sprinkles.

Huevos rancheros (*hoo-ay-voss ran-chair-os*)
A Mexican dish made from a fried egg and some spicy tomato sauce on a tortilla wrap.

Arepas (*ah-re-pah*)
These Colombian corn cakes are round and sometimes stuffed with cheese.

Ogi (*oh-gee*) **and akara**
In Nigeria, people eat maize porridge and fried black bean cakes.

11

HOME SWEET HOME
Where people live

There are a lot of different kinds of homes around the world.
Which one would you like to stay in?

A home on a lake
The Uru people of Peru and Bolivia live on Lake Titicaca. They make their homes on floating islands made of reeds.

A round home
Mongolian herder families live in round tents called *gers*. They take their homes with them when they travel around with their herds of animals.

A home on stilts
People live in homes on stilts in the mountains of Vietnam. The stilts keep the houses above the muddy ground when it rains.

A painted home
The Ndebele *(en-deb-ell-ay)* people of South Africa and Zimbabwe decorate the mud walls of their homes with beautiful bright patterns.

A snowy home
Nenet families live in the snowy far north of Russia. They move around, following their reindeer herds through the snow. They set up their reindeer skin tents wherever they go.

A cave home
Families have made their homes in caves in Göreme, Turkey, for hundreds of years.

A shared home
Dayak families live in the Borneo jungle. They share a longhouse — a home where lots of families live together. Each family has its own space in the longhouse.

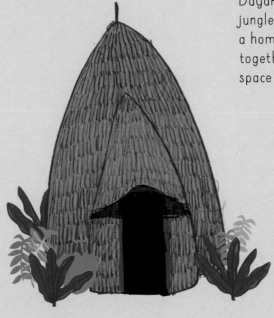

A tall home
The Dorze people live in the mountains of Ethiopia. They build their tall, round homes from bamboo and banana leaves.

HOME DECORATIONS

Mongolian *gers* usually have a blue sash hanging up inside, believed to bring the family peace and happiness.

British homes are sometimes decorated with a horseshoe (hung so it looks like a 'U'), for good luck.

In Singapore, it's traditional to roll a pineapple into a new home, to bring good fortune.

Colourful decorated bamboo rakes called *kumade (coo-mah-day)* are often hung in Japanese homes to gather good luck.

HELLO, NONNA!

Names for your family

Italy – nonna and nonno

Sweden – mormor and morfar
(mother's parents)
farmor and farfar
(father's parents)

Iceland – amma and afi *(ah-vay)*

Japan – obaasan *(oh-baah-sahn)*
and sofu *(so-foo)*

GRANDMAS AND GRANDADS

Grandmas and grandads are awesome right across the planet! Here are some names for them around the world.

Croatia – baka and deda

Greece – yaya and papou *(pah-poo)*

Philippines – lola and lolo

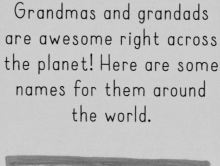

Poland – babcia *(bab-cha)*
and dziadek *(jah-deck)*

Finland – mummo *(moo-ma)* and ukki *(oo-kee)*

Estonia – ema and isa *(ee-sah)*

Belarus – maci *(ma-che)* and baćka *(bach-ka)*

Germany – mami and papi

MUMS AND DADS

Here's what mums and dads are called in some countries.

Indonesia – ibu and ayah

Turkey – anne *(ah-ney)* and baba

Denmark – mor and far

Samoa – tina and tama

Albania – motēr and vëlla

Ireland – deirfiur *(dri-foor)* and deartháir *(dhrih-hawr)*

Netherlands – zus *(zoos)* and broer *(broo-er)*

SISTERS AND BROTHERS

Here are some world names to try out on brothers and sisters.

Finland – sisko and veli

Romania – sora and frate *(frar-tay)*

ANIMAL FRIENDS

Pets around the planet

Lots of children have pets. Which one would you like to love and look after?

Parrot
People who live in the South American Amazon sometimes keep tame parrots around their rainforest homes.

Japanese bobtail cat
In Japan, bobtail cats are considered lucky pets. Instead of a long tail a bobtail cat has a small one like a rabbit.

Pet rock
People in the USA once bought these beach pebbles as pets, just for fun. They came in a box with their own straw and they never needed feeding!

Hedgehog
In Vietnam, it's not unusual to keep a hedgehog as a house pet.

Arowana fish
In China, the arowana fish is a lucky pet, thought to bring wealth and happiness to its owner. The rarest arowana fish can cost £80,000 or more!

Rhino beetle
Rhino beetles are popular pets in South Korea, where people feed them a special beetle jelly.

Rat
Rats are clever, clean pets. In the Karni Mata Temple in India, thousands of rats are looked after as holy animals and given treats such as milk and coconut.

Racing pigeon
Racing pigeons are popular pets in Middle Eastern countries such as Kuwait and Dubai. The pigeons are trained to fly home from wherever they are released.

Singing cricket
In Japan and China, some people like to keep singing crickets as pets. The crickets don't really sing, though. They rub their wings together to make a noise.

Alpaca
In Peru, children are sometimes given baby alpacas to look after. Once the alpacas grow up they live in herds, grazing outdoors.

Make up names for the pets on these pages.

BE HAPPY!

Words to say when you're smiling

Fill a room with happiness every morning. Stretch your arms out wide, smile and say the word "happy" loudly in a different language.

Swahili
(spoken in countries
in East Africa)
FURAHA
foo-ra-ha

Turkish
MUTLU
mut-low

French
JOYEUX
jw-eye-euh

German
GLÜCKLICH
gluh-clish

Italian
FELICE
fel-ee-chay

Hindi
(spoken in India)

KHUSH

khush

Portuguese

FELIZ

fell-eez

Arabic

MABSOOT

mab-suit

Indonesian

SENANG

se-nang

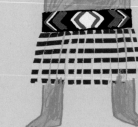

Maori
(spoken in New Zealand)

OAOA

oh-ah-oh-ah

Albanian

I LUMTUR

ee loom-tor

Gaelic
(spoken in Ireland)

SÁSTA

sa-sta

19

TIME TO GO TO SCHOOL
Journeys in different countries

Travelling to school isn't the same for everyone. Some children go to school...

...by school bus
In the USA, nearly half a million children catch a school bus every day. The school buses are famous for being painted yellow.

...in a rickshaw
In some parts of India, children go to school in a rickshaw with a driver pedaling at the front.

...by boat
Children go to school by rowing boat on the Tonlé Sap lake in Cambodia. They live in homes on stilts on the lake, and their school is on stilts, too.

...on foot
Many children who live in the African countryside walk or run to school. Some have to trek for miles to get to their lessons.

...by zipwire
Some Colombian children must cross the Rio Negro river on a zipwire to get to their school in Los Piños.

...in a tuk-tuk
In Sri Lanka and Thailand, children often go to school by *tuk-tuk*, a motorbike taxi with three wheels.

...by underground train
Japanese children often travel from home to school by underground train.

...by donkey
It's hard for disabled children to get to school in the African countryside, so in Eritrea the charity UNICEF has given disabled children donkeys to help carry them to their lessons.

...by ladder
The children of Zhang Jiawan in southern China must climb steep ladders up a cliff to get to their school.

...by bicycle
In the Netherlands, a lot of children go to school by bicycle — more than any other country in the world.

How do you get to school?

DRESSED FOR SCHOOL
School uniforms around the world

Here are some of the clothes that children wear to school.

Hats and scarves
In Muslim schools in Malaysia, girls wear a long headscarf called a *tudung (too-dung)* and a long top and skirt called a *baju kurung (ba-joo kur-ong)*. Boys wear a cap called a *songkok*.

Woolly warm clothes
The Quechua *(kay-choo-wa)* People live high in the Andes Mountains of South America. They wear their colourful warm everyday clothes, made of llama wool, to school. Girls wear an upturned *montera* hat and woolly jacket called a *jobona*. Boys wear a poncho and a woolly beanie hat called a *chullo (choo-yo)*.

Tops and trousers
Pakistani girls usually wear a long top with trousers to school. Their outfit is called a *shalwar kameez (sal-wa kam-eez)*.

Sailor clothes
Japanese school uniforms are often based on the clothes that sailors wore a hundred years ago. The girls have a sailor top and skirt. The boys have a suit with shiny buttons down the front.

22

Computer uniform

Children in the Brazilian city of Vitória da Conquista don't need to have a class register in the morning. Instead they have computer chips fitted on their school shirts. When they get to school a computer scans the chip and records them arriving.

Skirts for everyone

Some Tongan schoolboys wear a traditional wraparound skirt called a *tupenu* (too-peh-noo), with a wraparound mat called a *ta'ovala* (ta-oo-va-la) on top. Tongan girls usually wear a pinafore to school but they sometimes put a ta'ovala on top.

School robes

In Southeast Asia, some children go to Buddhist monastery schools. They have ordinary school lessons and also learn the Buddhist religion. They wear orange robes, which Buddhist monks have worn for hundreds of years.

School patterns

Children in Indonesia sometimes wear patterned shirts decorated in a style called *batik* (bat-eek). Each school has its own special batik design.

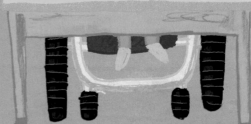

MY CLASSROOM
Where we learn

We all learn in different kinds of classrooms. Where would you like to learn?

In the world's biggest school
The City Montessori School in Lucknow, India, has 55,000 pupils and over 1,000 classrooms dotted around the town.

Up a mountain
At Sun Peaks in Canada children go by ski lift to their school on top of a mountain. They ski back home at the end of the day.

In a grass hut
Some children in hot countries have their classrooms in grass huts.

School words
Here are some school words from around the world. Try using one yourself!

OPETTAJA
(op-eh-tie-ya)
"Teacher" in Finnish

KOOL
"School" in Estonian

STUNDE
(sh-tun-da)
"Lesson" in German

Outdoors
Children in hot countries sometimes have their lessons sitting outside.

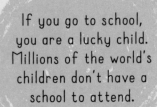

If you go to school, you are a lucky child. Millions of the world's children don't have a school to attend.

In a bus
In the city of Hyderabad in India, poor children cannot get to school, so the school comes to them. It's called the School on Wheels because the classroom is set up in a bus.

In the School of the Air
Some Australian children live many hundreds of miles from school. Instead they join the School of the Air. Their home is their classroom, and they speak to their teachers and classmates by two-way radio or via a computer.

On the floor
In some village schools around the world, there might not be chairs or desks. The children sit on mats on the floor instead.

What we learn ...

Children in South India learn a sport called *mallakhamb*. It's a kind of gymnastics performed around a long wooden pole.

In some Chinese and Mongolian schools children learn calligraphy. They are taught to paint letters beautifully with a brush and ink.

Some Chinese children learn martial arts every day as well as doing schoolwork.

Some Norwegian schools have a yearly Ski Day. Children go outdoors with their teachers to learn skiing instead of having indoor lessons.

THIRSTY?

Drinks around the world

All of this is thirsty work!
Which one of these drinks would you like to try?

Iced tea — cha yen
On the streets of Thailand you might see people buying *cha yen* from a motorbike drink cart. It's made of tea, condensed milk and spices.

Mint tea — té moruno (*tay mor-oo-no*)
In Morocco, this sugary minty tea is poured from up high into little glass cups. The higher the tea-maker pours, the more important the guest. The King of Morocco's official tea-pourers have been known to stand on ladders to pour a royal drink.

Aniseed milk — anijsmelk (*an-es-melk*)
Before you go to bed in the Netherlands, you might be given a mug of this warm milk that tastes of licorice-flavoured aniseed. It's supposed to help you sleep.

Pickled cabbage water — kimchi drink
Spicy pickled cabbage called *kimchi* is popular in South Korea. The drink is the cloudy juice left over from making the cabbage.

Fruit mix — spris
Would you like a striped fruity smoothie? Then try an Ethiopian *spris*. It is made with layers of avocado, mango and papaya poured on top of each other.

Yoghurt drink — lassi
All over India you can buy a cup of *lassi*, yoghurt mixed with water and spices. It can taste salty or sweet.

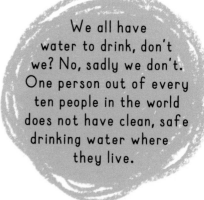

We all have water to drink, don't we? No, sadly we don't. One person out of every ten people in the world does not have clean, safe drinking water where they live.

Chocolate corn drink — champurrado (*cham-purr-ah-doh*)
You can buy a cup of this warming sweet drink on the streets of Mexico. It's made from corn flour, sugar, vanilla, cinnamon and yummy melted chocolate.

WORDS FOR HOORAY!

Cheering words

It feels good to cheer in any language.
All together now. One, two, three . . .

Italian
EVVIVA!
eh-veev-a

Swedish
HEJA !
hey-ya

Japanese
YATTAAA !
ya-ta

Afrikaans
(spoken in South Africa)
GELUK!
hel-ook

Lithuanian
VALIO!
val-ee-oh

Bosnian
URA !
oo-ra

TOP TO TOE

Clothes for your head and feet

Which hat or pair of shoes would you like to wear? You could even try some face painting, too.

THE WORLD HAT SHOP

A bowler hat from Bolivia

A Ukranian flower crown called a *vinok* (vee-nok)

A beaded hat worn by *Hmong* (mong) women in Thailand

A *kofia* hat from Kenya

A *bush* hat from Australia

A *keffiyeh* (kef-ee-ya) scarf worn in the Middle East

A Vietnamese *nón lá* straw hat

A *dhaka topi* (da-ka toe-pee) hat from Nepal

A *pakol* hat from Afghanistan

A head wrap from Africa (there are lots of different ways to tie it)

ANHYGOEL!
(an-hug-oil)
"Amazing!" in Welsh

What special hats do people wear in your country?

THE WORLD SHOE SHOP

Indian *jutti* (joo-tee) shoes

Greek *tsarouhi* (sar-oo-hi) shoes

Tshoglham (show-lam) boots from Bhutan

Scottish ghillie (ghill-ee) dancing shoes

Finnish Sámi skaller boots

Moroccan babouche (bab-ooch) shoes

Mongolian gutul (goo-tal) boots

Spanish espadrille (ess-pah-dree-yeh) sandals

US cowboy boots

Peruvian *hojotas* (oh-ho-ta), made from recycled tyres

FACE ART

Some children live in communities where people decorate their skin, especially on festival days. Here are three different styles.

A child of the Kayapo people, who live in Brazil

A child of the Omo people, who live in Ethiopia

A child of the Sepik people, who live in Papua New Guinea

MAC, MAC, BUN, BUN!

Noises animals make

Most of us learn animal noises when we are small, but we say them differently. Try some international noises and pick your favourites!

Cats go...
meo meo in Vietnam
nyan nyan in Japan
nǎu nǎu in Estonia
nyaong nyaong in
South Korea

Owls go...
hoo hoo in Pakistan
brrbr brrbr in Syria
uh uh uh in Russia
huhuu in Finland

Ducks go...
rap rap in Denmark
coin coin in France
mac mac in Romania
krya krya in Russia

Bees go...
sum sum in Germany
wing wing in South Korea
bun bun in Japan
zoum zoum in Greece

Dogs go...
ab hab in **Tunisia**
ham ham in **Albania**
hev hev in **Turkey**
guk guk in **Indonesia**

Mice go...
piep piep in the **Netherlands**
pip pip in **Sweden**
zi zi in **China**
squitt squitt in **Italy**

Cows go...
buu in the **Czech Republic**
ammuu in **Finland**
hamba in **Bangladesh**
umboo in **Mongolia**

Frogs go...
ribbit ribbit in the
United Kingdom
kum kum in **Poland**
brekeke in **Hungary**
op op in **Thailand**

Cockerels go...
cocorococo in **Portugal**
kuklooku in **Pakistan**
kikiriki in **Spain**
ko ko koi in **Taiwan**

JOIN THE WORLD BAND
Playing music

Here are some musical instruments from around the world.
Which one would you choose to play in a world band?

Some river rocks
In Hawaii, dancers sometimes tap river rocks
together as they do a hula dance. To play river rocks
you need four smooth flat pebbles, two in each hand.
You could use beach pebbles if you wanted.
Here's how to make a sound with them.
1. Hold one pebble between your thumb and forefinger.
2. Put the other pebble on your palm.
3. Click the two pebbles together.

Nose music
In the northern
Philippines, some people
are expert at playing
a nose flute called the
pitung ilong. To play
it you must blow
through your nose into
a tube of bamboo.

An ugly stick
Newfoundland is an island off the
coast of Canada. People there make
their own ugly sticks to play along
to music. They nail bottle tops, bells
and tin cans to a broom handle and
stick a rubber boot on the bottom.
Then they bang the cans and bottle
tops with a wooden spoon and stomp
the boot on the ground.

A shell
Big conch shells are played like trumpets in places around the world where the shells are found in the ocean, such as New Zealand. The end of the shell is cut off to make the mouthpiece. You can put your hand into the shell to change the notes.

A cactus
A Chilean rain stick is made from a dried cactus stalk with cactus prickles pressed into it and seeds put inside. To play a rain stick you need to shake it to make a sound like falling raindrops. It's said to magically make real rain fall!

A leaf
Some Australian Aboriginal people can make music with a gum leaf. They blow across the leaf to make notes.

Some seed pods
In the Congo, drummers wear *nsakala* (n-sack-a-la) on their wrists as they drum. The nsakala are round dried seed pods as big as tennis balls, filled with seeds that rattle along to the drumming music.

MY TUMMY'S RUMBLING

It must be lunchtime

We might eat different lunches around the world, but we all have rumbling tummies sometimes! Which school lunch would you like to eat when you're hungry?

Miso soup, rice, fish and pickled salad
In Japan, children usually have lunches cooked for them at school. They eat their lunch in their own classroom with their teacher, helping to serve it out and cleaning up afterwards.

Vegetable stew, some rice and a piece of flatbread
Children in southern Asia often take a stack of tiffin boxes full of lunch to school. Each metal tiffin box carries a different part of the lunch.

Beef stew, rice and beans, salad, fruit and bread
A lot of the food in Brazilian schools is bought from local farmers and bakers. Brazil made this a law so that children's food would be healthy and fresh.

Rice, some *sambar* (a stew made of lentils), vegetable stir fry, curd (like yoghurt), sweet semolina pudding called *kesari*
Children in southern India would get this kind of school meal laid out on a *thali* (tar-lee) plate, which has different sections for each food. They would usually eat it with their fingers, sitting on the floor.

LUNCH TIME

Fish soup, fried rice with tofu, fermented cabbage called *kimchi*, soybean sprouts, and fruit
In South Korea, pupils and teachers usually sit together to eat lunch, and the pupils help to clean up afterwards.

Pasta (a different kind every day), meat with a side of vegetables, and fruit
Italian schoolchildren often get cooked three-course meals at lunchtime.

Rice and spicy bean stew with some flatbread
This is a popular lunch all over Africa. In Nigeria, the bean stew is called *ewa agoyin* (ay-wah ah-go-yin). It's cooked with onions, peppers and different spices.

Beetroot soup called *borsch*, pickled cabbage, sausage and mashed potatoes, sweet pancake and fruit
In Ukraine, children usually have around 30 minutes for lunch in school.

Delicious is . . .

DADI!
in Hausa
(Spoken in Nigeria and Chad)

DELICIOSO!
in Brazilian

LAZAT!
in Malay
(Spoken in Malaysia)

SVADISHTA!
(*sva-dish-t*)
in Hindi
(Spoken in India)

DUZHE SMACHNYY!
(*doo-za smach-nay*)
in Ukrainian

OISHII!
in Japanese

DELIZIOSO!
in Italian

MASHISOYO!
in Korean

Hic!
Hic!
Hic!
Hic!

CURES FOR HICCUPS

How do you try to stop your hiccups? Here are some different ideas from around the world.

A cure from Trinidad and Tobago
Stick a scrap of paper to your forehead using spit.

A cure from Norway
Swallow a spoonful of sugar and let the sugar grains trickle down your throat.

A cure from the USA
Eat a teaspoonful of peanut butter.

A cure from the UK
Make the person who is hiccupping jump by suddenly saying "Boo!"

A cure from India
Chew on a piece of fresh ginger.

A cure from Mexico
Stick a spit-covered piece of red string to your forehead.

A cure from the Dominican Republic
If a baby gets the hiccups, put a hair from the mother's head on the baby's forehead.

STOP IRONING MY HEAD!

Sayings around the world

Do you know some special sayings that people use where you live?
Try using some of these.

"He has a wide face" means
"He has a lot of friends" in Japanese

"You have a stick in your ear" means
"You are not listening properly" in Danish

"The cat is trapped" means
"Something's wrong" in Spanish

"Stop ironing my head" means
"Stop annoying me" in Armenian

"I have a cockroach" means
"I am feeling sad" in French

"**Some days honey, some days onions**" means
"You win some, you lose some" in Arabic

"**Don't feed the donkey sponge cake**" means
"Don't treat someone who doesn't
deserve it" in Portuguese

"**He is walking like a cat around hot porridge**" means
"He is avoiding saying something" in Norwegian

"**The carrots are cooked**" means
"There's nothing more you can do" in French

"**You have tomatoes on your eyes**" means
"You can't see what everyone else
can see" in German

"**Coat after rain**" means
"It's no good moaning now. It's
too late" in Hungarian

"**There is no cow on the ice**" means
"There's no need to worry" in Swedish

ATISHOO!
Words for sneezing

We don't all say the same words when we hear someone sneezing.
Here are some sneeze sayings from around the world.

Make a wish
Mexican people make a wish for someone who sneezes. The wish they make depends on how many sneezes there are.

1 ... **SALUD!**
"Health!"

2 ... **DINERO!**
"Money!"

3 ... **AMOR!**
"Love!"

Three sneezes!
If somebody sneezes three times, Dutch people say: *"Morgen mooi weer!"* It means: "The weather will be nice tomorrow." The three sneezes are supposed to be a sign of sunshine to come.

AtisHoo!

AtisHoo!

Someone's talking about you
If you sneeze once in Japan it's a sign that somebody is saying something nice about you. If you sneeze twice, it's a sign that somebody is saying something bad about you.

Be patient
If somebody hears you sneeze in Iran they might say: *"Sabr umad!"* (*sabber oom-ad*). It means "Patience has arrived." The person who has sneezed must now be patient and wait a minute or two before they do anything.

GESUNDHEIT!
(*ges-oond-hite*)
"Health!" in German

THUTHUKA!
(*to-koo-kah*)
"Grow!" in Zulu
(spoken in southern Africa)

NDO!
(*en-do*)
"Sorry!" in Igbo
(spoken in Nigeria)

EVVIVA!
(*eh-veev-a*)
"Hooray!" in Maltese

À TES SOUHAITS
(*a-tay-sway*)
"May your dreams come true" in French

PROSIT!
(*proh-zit*)
"Bless you" in Danish

DEUS TE ABAFE!
(*day-oos chee ab-ar-fee*)
"May God put a blanket over you" in Portuguese

MY TOOTH CAME OUT!

What to do next

When a wobbly tooth comes out, what should you do?
Children do different things around the world.

Throw it on the roof

If you are in Greece you should throw your tooth up on a roof and ask a magical little mouse for a new one. You'll need to make a wish:
"Little mouse, take my tooth. Give me a strong new one instead."

Throw it to the Sun

In Middle Eastern countries, throw your tooth at the Sun and ask it to give you back a bright new tooth.

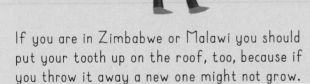

If you are in Zimbabwe or Malawi you should put your tooth up on the roof, too, because if you throw it away a new one might not grow.

In Sri Lanka, throw your tooth on the roof and ask a squirrel to bring you a new one.

Leave it for the mouse

In Spain, France, Italy and countries in South America, put your tooth under your pillow. A little mouse will come for it and leave you money. The tooth mouse has different names around the world. In Spain, Ratoncito Pérez will look after your tooth and in France, La Petite Souris will do it.

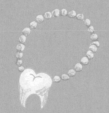

Make some jewellery

In Costa Rica, mothers sometimes make their children's teeth into little jewellery charms to hang on a necklace or a bracelet.

Leave it for the fairy

The tooth fairy visits lots of countries. If you are in North America, the United Kingdom, Australia or New Zealand, put your tooth under your pillow. The tooth fairy will take it and leave you some money.

Leave it for a rabbit

In El Salvador, pop your tooth under the pillow. A rabbit will come for it and leave you money.

HOORAY! IT'S KIDS' DAY!

Celebrations for children

Some days of the year are set aside especially for children.

A day when kids rule

April 23rd is Children's Day in Turkey. It's called *Çocuk Bayrami* (*show-jook bay-rah-me*). Children get to sit in Turkey's parliament alongside the adults, and pretend to rule for the day. Across Turkey children dress up in national costume and take part in celebrations.

A day for fishy friends

March 5th is Children's Day in Japan. It's called *Kodomo no Hi* (*koe-doe-moe no hee*). On Children's Day families put a pole outside their home decorated with streamers that look like carp fish. Carp fish are said to be strong and brave, and will bring good luck to the children of the family.

A day for dolls

March 3rd is the Doll Festival in Japan. It's called *Hina Matsuri* (*hee-na mat soor-ee*), and it's a day especially for daughters. Family dolls representing Japanese rulers of the past are put out on display, to bring daughters good luck. The smartly dressed dolls sit on a tall red stand, with the Emperor and Empress of the dolls on the top.

A day for fun

June 1st is Children's Day in China. Everyone gets the day off school, and it's a time for fun and treats. Nobody gets any homework on that day.

A day for brothers and sisters

In India, Mauritius and Nepal, there's an important festival for brothers and sisters, called *Raksha Bandhan (rack-sha band-an)*. It's a day for brothers and sisters to show how much they love each other, and they hold a special ceremony together. It takes place in August on a different date each year, for people who follow the Hindu religion.

First the sister ties a thread bracelet called a *rakhi (rah-kee)* on her brother's wrist. She says a prayer to wish him a long life. Then she marks his forehead with a red mark called a *tilak (tih-luhk)*.

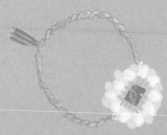

Now it's the brother's turn. He promises he will always help and protect his sister, come what may, and he gives her a gift. His sister gives him some delicious sweets to eat in return.

A girl can give a male friend a rakhi to wear if she doesn't have a brother.

A day for dressing up

The children of Trinidad and Tobago have their own Children's Carnival in springtime, just before the Christian festival of Easter. They spend months getting their costumes just right for the big procession in the town of Port of Spain.

GOOD LUCK, EVERYBODY
Being lucky or unlucky

What do you think is lucky or unlucky?
Do you recognise some of these beliefs from different countries?

For good luck in Brazil, leave a pot of salt in the corner of a room.

If your eye twitches it could be good luck in India. If you're a boy, a twitching right eye is good luck. If you're a girl, a twitching left eye is good luck.

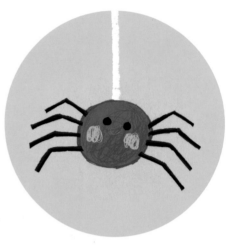

In Japan, if you see a spider in the morning, it means you'll have good luck. If you see it in the afternoon, you'll have bad luck.

Eight is a lucky number in China. When the Olympic Games were held there in 2008 the Games began on the eighth day of the eighth month, at eight minutes past eight in the evening, to bring good luck.

If a bird poops on you, your home or your car, it means you'll have good luck in Russia.

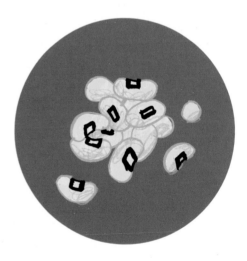

Sometimes people in the southern USA eat black-eyed peas on New Year's Day for good luck.

Red is the colour of good luck in Asian countries.

Orange is a lucky colour in Buddhist countries such as Bhutan.

Green is the colour of good luck in the Middle East.

LUCKY NEW YEAR

People in Denmark like to jump off chairs, pretending they are jumping into the New Year.

Spanish people eat 12 grapes for good luck as the clock strikes twelve on New Year's Eve.

People in Brazil wear yellow underwear on New Year's Eve for good luck, while Italians like to wear lucky red underwear.

THAT'S UNLUCKY

In Thailand, it's unlucky to whistle in the dark, in case you wake up bad spirits.

The number four is unlucky in China, so high-rise buildings don't have a fourth floor. The floor numbers go straight from three to five.

In Hawaii, it's unlucky to take a banana onboard a boat. It would bring bad luck on your trip.

The number 13 is unlucky in the United Kingdom. If anybody books a table for 13 people at the Savoy Hotel in London, a cat statue called Kaspar is sat at their table to make the number of guests up to 14.

In India, it's unlucky to cut your nails or hair on a Saturday, in case you upset the Hindu god, Shani.

White is an unlucky colour in China.

Green is an unlucky colour in Indonesia.

LET'S PLAY!
The world's toybox

Which toy would you like to borrow?

A toy to make you taller
In Indonesia, children play on stilts made of bamboo sticks, called *egrang (err-kran)*. Sometimes they have egrang races.

A car made of fruit
Children in Indonesia love to make toy cars from a fruit called a *jeruk bali (jerook-balee)*, which is like a grapefruit. The skin of the fruit makes the parts of the car and strips of coconut hold them together.

Tiny dolls to take away your worries
Guatemalan worry dolls are only tiny but if you put them under your pillow they are said to take your worries away.

A doll to protect you
Handmade cloth *motanka (mo-tanko)* dolls are given to children in Ukraine to protect them from bad luck. The dolls don't have faces. A motanka with a face is thought to be unlucky.

A toy to swing on
Every year in Nepal, children get a new toy — a *ping* swing made from bamboo poles and grass ropes. Ping swings are built in lots of villages around the country for everyone to enjoy during the Hindu religious festival of Dashain.

A rag doll for everyone

In Russia, children have lucky faceless rag dolls, too. Which one would you like? You could choose from a *pelenashka* (peh-leh-nash-ka) baby doll, a *moskovka* (mus-kov-ka) doll with six mini children or perhaps a *desyatiruchka* (dis-yat-ee-rooch-ka) doll who has ten hands for doing lots of housework.

A toy to spin

A *trompo* is a Mexican wooden top that you can spin around by pulling on a string. Two trompos can fight. The winner knocks the other one over.

A toy to make you think

Lots of African countries have versions of the game *mancala*. It's played on a wooden board with bowls carved out of it, like an egg box. Players move seeds or pebbles around and try to capture their opponent's pieces.

A toy to make you dance

In Java, you'll sometimes see children riding a toy horse cut from a bamboo mat and painted brightly. They are playing at *kuda lumping* (koo-da lum-ping), a traditional horse-riding dance that you would see performed at Javan parades and ceremonies.

A car made of everything

Kenyan children make their own toy cars, called *galimoto*. They use wire to make the car body and they add all sorts of extras such as sticks, cornstalks and recycled bits and pieces.

MY TURN!
Playtime games

Which round-the-world playtime game would you like to try?

Ant, human, elephant
Have you ever played the game *Rock, Paper, Scissors*? Here's a similar game that children play in Indonesia. It's called *Semut, Orang, Gajah* (ant, human, elephant). Two people stand in front of each other and use these hand signs.

Semut beats gajah. An ant could crawl into the elephant's ear and tickle it.
Orang beats semut. A human could step on an ant.
Gajah beats orang. An elephant could squash a human.

Semut (*suh-moot*)
Point your little finger at your friend's hand.

Orang (*orr-ahng*)
Point your first finger at your friend's hand.

Gajah (*gha-jah*)
Point your thumb at your friend's hand.

Knee jumping
Traditional Inuit games are designed to make people strong and fit. Try an Inuit knee jump at home.

1. Kneel on the floor with your toes straight out behind you.

2. Swing your arms back and get read to hop. You'll need to use your tummy muscles to help you.

3. Jump forward and land on your feet. See how far you can get.

Jianzi

People of all ages like to play jianzi (*chee-an-zee*) in China. The jianzi is a shuttlecock made of little plastic discs with feathers attached to it. The game is to keep the jianzi off the ground for as long as you can without using your arms. You could use a small beanbag for the game instead of a jianzi shuttlecock.

Lucky laugh

Everybody plays this game on New Year's Day in Japan. It's called *fukuwarai* (*foo-coo wa-ri*). Its name means lucky laugh, and it makes everybody giggle.

1. To play, you need a large drawing of a blank face. Fix it to the wall or lay it on the floor.

2. Cut out two eyes, a nose and a mouth from old magazines. Put some blobs of sticky putty on the back of each one. Now you're ready for the game.

3. Each player takes it in turn to be blindfolded. They must try to stick the eyes, nose and mouth somewhere on the face while everybody else calls out suggestions. When the player has finished they get to see their funny face, and then pass the blindfold on to somebody else for a turn.

Ampe

Ampe (*ahm-pay*) is a traditional game played in Ghana.

1. Find someone to play with and face each other. Decide who is Player 1 and who is Player 2.

2. Jump, clap and push one leg forward.

3. If you push your legs forward opposite each other, Player 1 gets a point.

4. If you push legs forward that are not opposite to each other, Player 2 gets a point.

The winner is the first player to get to ten points.

MMMM... CAKE!

Yummy cakes from around the world

Which one would you like to try first?

Cat cake
Lussekats (loo-seh kot-er) from Sweden are buns dotted with raisins and flavoured with a spice called saffron. They are eaten on December 13th, which is St Lucia's Day in Sweden. The name of the bun means "Lucia's cat". Do you think the s-shaped bun looks like a curled-up cat?

Bone cake
Spanish *huesos de santo (hoo-ay-soss de santo)* are eaten on November 1st, which is a Christian festival called All Saints' Day. The cakes are tubes of white marzipan filled with custard. Do they remind you of something? Here's a clue: their name means "saint's bones"!

Moon cake
Mooncakes from China are little round cakes filled with bean paste and decorated with Chinese symbols that represent long life. They are eaten during the Mid-Autumn Festival to celebrate the moon.

New Year's Eve cake
On New Year's Eve, people in Japan love to eat *mochi (moh-chee)*, little balls of rice paste flavoured with red bean paste. In springtime, they eat pink mochi that represent the beautiful cherry blossom on Japanese trees.

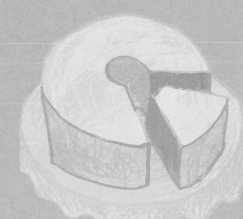

Leaf cake
The Malaysian *pandan chiffon (pan-dan shiff-on)* cake could be the brightest green sponge you'll ever see. It gets its colour from the sweet juice of pandanus palm leaves used in the cake mixture.

Tree cake
The French *bûche de Noël (boosh de no-ell)* is a chocolate cake shaped like a log from a tree. It represents a very ancient custom when people burned a special log in their home to mark the end of winter.

Are special traditional cakes ever eaten where you live?

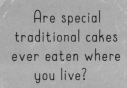

Baby cake
On January 6th, everybody eats king cake in New Orleans, USA. Somewhere hidden inside each brightly coloured cake there is a tiny plastic baby representing the baby Jesus. Whoever gets the baby must buy the next cake.

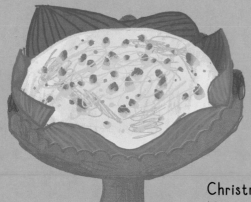

Christmas morning cake
If you found yourself in the Philippines on Christmas morning, you would be given a slice of *bibingka (bee-bing-ka)*, a coconut-flavoured rice pudding cake. Happy Christmas!

Egg cake
In some parts of Spain, lucky children get a *Mona de Pascua (moh-na de pas-qua)* cake at Eastertime. The cake has an egg on top for every year of the child's life. The eggs can be chocolate or real boiled eggs. Which one would you like?

Rice cake
South Korean *tteok (duck)* cakes are shaped and decorated to look like flowers, fruit or shells, and filled with different flavours. They are given as special gifts.

I CALL THIS SOCK...

Everyday words to try

Reinvent your world by renaming the things around you.
Pick a word you like and try using it.

Dog is ...
perro (pehr-ro) in Spanish
inu (ee-noo) in Japanese
koira (koy-ra) in Finnish

Cat is ...
kočka (koch-ka) in Czech
pusa (poo-sa) in Filipino
con mèo (con may-oh) in Vietnamese

Toilet is ...
twaletta (twa-let-ah) in Maltese
tandas (tahn-dahs) in Malay
toilette (twa-let) in French

Door is ...
vrata (ver-ah-tah) in Bosnian
doras in Irish
uks (ooks) in Estonian

Shoe is ...
ivava (ee-va-va) in Fijian
joota in Hindi
obuvka (ob-oov-ka) in Bulgarian

Sock is ...
calzino (cal-zee-no) in Italian
strumpa (stroom-pa) in Swedish
zokni (zok-nee) in Hungarian

Bed is ...
gwely (gwale-eugh) in Welsh
cama (cuh-ma) in Portuguese
chuáng (chwa-ang) in Chinese

Table is ...
taawleh (tar-well-ai) in Arabic
taflan in Icelandic
tafel (tar-fel) in Afrikaans

Chair is ...
stol in Norwegian
sandalye (sand-al-yay) in Turkish
stolica in Serbian

SURE!

Useful expressions to try

Here are some expressions you might find helpful and fun to use.

SIGUR!
(*see-goor*)
"Sure!" in Romanian

DE HOGY!
(*de-hog-ee*)
"No way!" in Hungarian

NOIOSO!
(*no-ee-oh-so*)
"Boring!" in Italian

WAS?
(*vas?*)
"What?" in German

BAH!
(*bar*)
"Yuck!" in Dutch

CHOMU?
(*cho-moo?*)
"Why?" in Ukranian

YOU LOOK GREAT!
Clothes for special occasions

Children might not wear clothes like these every day, but it can be fun to dress in special outfits sometimes.

Sparkly outfits
Everybody wears their best clothes to a wedding. In India, boys and girls usually have lots of sparkly embroidery on their wedding clothes.

Smart clothes
In West African countries, boys wear a *boubou* (*boo-boo*), a smart flowing robe, for special occasions. Girls wear their prettiest wraparound skirt, called *a pagne* (*pan-ya*).

Magical clothes
Many countries have a national costume which people wear on special celebration days. In Belarus, the national costume has a lot of red and black embroidery. The embroidered patterns were once thought to have magic powers that protected the wearer from harm.

Clothes for New Year
Mongolian people celebrate their New Year in February. Everybody wears their best *deel*, which is a wraparound top with a sash. The smartest deels are made of embroidered silk.

Clothes for dancing

Clothes for Irish dancing are embroidered with swirling patterns that copy the decoration found in old Irish books. The girls wear decorated dresses and the boys wear embroidered waistcoats.

Do you have any clothes you like to wear for special occasions?

Clothes for outdoors

The people of the Kashmir region in Southeast Asia wear an outdoor robe called *a pheran* (*fer-an*). In winter, they keep warm with a woolly pheran. On special occasions they wear smart embroidered pherans.

Clothes for keeping warm

The Nenets people need to keep warm in their chilly Siberian home. They wear thick coats and trousers made from reindeer skin. They might put on a parka (an overhead coat) called *a malitsa* (*mah-lit-sa*), or *a yagushka* (*yah-goosh-ka*) that buttons at the front and is furry inside and out.

Clothes made from plants

On special occasions, Hawaiian people wear *lei* (*lay*), beautiful neck wreaths made from flowers, leaves, seeds, nuts and feathers. The lei represents respect and love, and it's particularly popular on May 1st, Lei Day in Hawaii. Everyone has a holiday and celebrates Hawaii on that day.

HAPPY BIRTHDAY, WORLD
Party fun!

Every day it's somebody's birthday somewhere.
Let's celebrate!

Sometimes children with birthdays in Newfoundland (Canada) get their noses smeared with butter. The legend says that they will be too slippery for bad spirits to catch them.

In Mexico, the person with a birthday takes the first bite of their birthday cake, then gets their face pushed into it.

In Jamaica, anyone celebrating a birthday gets a bag of flour thrown at them.

On someone's birthday in Nepal, they get a red mark on their forehead. It's made of coloured rice yoghurt called *tikka* (tee-ka).

On somebody's birthday in Brazil, they get their earlobes pulled once for every year of their life. Ouch!

The second day of the Chinese New Year is celebrated as the birthday of all Chinese dogs.

In Hungary, people pull the earlobes of the person celebrating their birthday. They say "May your earlobes grow to your ankles." It means "May you have a long life."

IT'S FOR YOU!
Gifts people give

Giving somebody a gift is a great way to make them feel happy, wherever they live.

A visit from a witch
The good witch *La Befana* flies around Italy on her broomstick on the night of January 5th, wearing a pointy hat and an old patchwork coat. She leaves gifts of sweets for good children, but she leaves lumps of coal for naughty ones. Italian children sometimes leave out a note and a snack for her.

A poop log
In the area of Spain called Catalonia, children get some early Christmas presents from a funny little hollow log with a face, a red hat and a cloth covering its behind. Presents are hidden inside the log and come out of the back, so it's called a *caga tió*, which means "poop log"!

The Yule Cat
In Iceland, children are given new clothes on Christmas day. It's because of the legend of the Yule Cat, *Jólakötturinn* (*yole-a-cur-tin*). The story goes that the Yule Cat monster will come to eat them if they don't wear something new!

A hat full of sweets
In Azerbaijan in March, everybody celebrates a national holiday called *Novruz*. In the evening children leave bags or hats outside their neighbours' front doors. The neighbours fill the bags with sweets and small gifts.

SOME TRADITIONAL BIRTHDAY FOOD

In Australia, they eat fairy bread — buttered bread covered in coloured cake sprinkles.

In South Korea, they eat seaweed soup called *miyeok guk* (*me-ok gook*).

In China, they eat *yi-mein* (*yee-meen*)— skinny long noodles that represent long life.

HUNGRY AGAIN?

It's dinnertime

How different is your dinner from these?

In Jamaica, people tend to have dinner at 4-5pm . . .

. . . but in Spain people eat dinner at around 10pm in the evening.

In Australia and the USA, people like to cook dinner outside on a barbecue in summer.

The people of the Mongolian plains cook their dinners inside their *gers* (tents), in pots over a fire.

Some Amazonian tribes live deep in the Amazon rainforest that stretches across South America. For their food, they hunt animals and gather plants to eat. Their meals depend on the creatures they can catch and the plants they gather during the day.

People in East African countries often have *ugali* *(ooh-gar-lee)* with their meal. It's a thick dough made from maize flour and water, and it's good for dipping into stews.

Nearly half the world eats rice as their main food of the day, especially in Asia.

Some religions around the world have eating rules. In India, lots of people do not eat meat because of their religious beliefs. They make delicious vegetable dishes for dinner instead. Jewish and Muslim people do not eat pork.

If you have breakfast, lunch and dinner then you are a lucky person. Many millions of the world's children might only have one small meal a day.

57

ALWAYS TWIRL YOUR SPAGHETTI

Manners for everyone

There are lots of different ways to be polite around the world.

If you are in Thailand, don't touch somebody's head, unless you know them very well. Otherwise it's disrespectful.

If you are in a country in the Far East, don't leave your chopsticks sticking up in a bowl of rice. It's unlucky.

If you are in Italy, don't cut up your spaghetti. That's bad manners. Twirl it round a fork to eat it instead.

In India, parts of Africa and the Middle East, it's rude to eat food with your left hand.

If you are in Egypt, don't sprinkle salt on food you are given. It's an insult to the person who made you the food.

THAT'S RUDE

In Ethiopia, people eat with their hands and they sometimes feed each other. They give each other a *gursha* (a mouthful). It's an honour to get a gursha and you should give one back.

It's a good idea to ask people to tell you the rules of politeness in their country. That way you won't be rude by mistake.

If you are eating in China, leave a few leftovers on the plate when you have finished. It shows that your host has given you plenty of food.

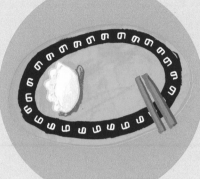

If someone older than you comes to visit in India, put your palms together and bow down. They will be pleased that you are showing them respect.

If you drop some bread on the floor in Afghanistan, you can pick it up, kiss it, place it to your forehead and put it back on your plate. It shows respect for your food.

Slurp when you are eating noodles in Japan. It shows how delicious the food is.

THAT'S POLITE

Italian
ARRIVEDERCI
ar-ee-va-dare-chee

Slovenian
SE VIDIMO
say vid-imo

Danish
VI SES SNART
vee-say-snart

Malay
JUMPA LAGI
joom-pa lagi

(spoken in countries
in Southeast Asia)

**SEE YOU
SOON!**

Uzbek
KO'RISHGUNCHA
koor-ish-gun-cha

(spoken in
Uzbekistan)

Jamaican patois
LIKKLE MUORE
lick-l muir-ee

Filipino
**HANG GANG
SA MULI**
hang-gang sa mooli

(spoken in the Philippines)

Greek
TA LÉMÉ SYNTOMA
ta le-may sin-toe-ma

Norwegian
HADET
har-de

Farsi
KHODA HAFEZ
coh-da haf-ez

(spoken in Iran)

GOODBYE!

Turkish
GÜLE GÜLE
gu-lay gu-lay

Fijian
MOCE
moth-ey

Hawaiian
ALOHA
al-oh-hah
(the same word
means hello!)

Bulgarian
DOVIJDANE
dov-ish-dun-ay

Japanese
SAYONARA
sai-oh-nar-ah

Polish
DO WIDZENIA
do vid-zen-ya

Belarusian
DA PABAČEŃNYA
da pa-ba-chen-ya

NORTH and
CENTRAL
AMERICA

SOUTH
AMERICA

AFRIC

ANTARCTICA

ROPE

ASIA

OCEANIA

POINT
TO WHERE
YOU LIVE!

63

List of countries featured

Afghanistan
Albania
Andorra
Armenia
Australia
Azerbaijan
Bali
Bangladesh
Belarus
Bhutan
Bolivia
Borneo
Bosnia and Herzegovina
Brazil
Bulgaria
Burkino Faso
Cambodia
Canada
Chile
China
Colombia
Congo
Costa Rica
Croatia

Czech Republic
Denmark
Dominican Republic
Egypt
El Salvador
Estonia
Ethiopia
Fiji
Finland
France
Germany
Ghana
Greece
Guatemala
Hawaii
Hungary
Iceland
India
Indonesia
Iran
Ireland
Italy
Jamaica
Japan

Java
Kenya
Lithuania
Malawi
Malaysia
Malta
Mauritius
Mexico
Mongolia
Morocco
Nigeria
Nepal
Netherlands
New Zealand
Norway
Pakistan
Papua New Guinea
Peru
Philippines
Poland
Portugal
Romania
Russia
Samoa

Serbia
Singapore
Slovenia
South Africa
South Korea
Spain
Sri Lanka
Sweden
Syria
Taiwan
Thailand
Tonga
Trinidad and Tobago
Tunisia
Turkey
Ukraine
United Kingdom (England,
Northern Ireland,
Scotland and Wales)
USA
Uzbekistan
Venezuela
Vietnam
Zimbabwe

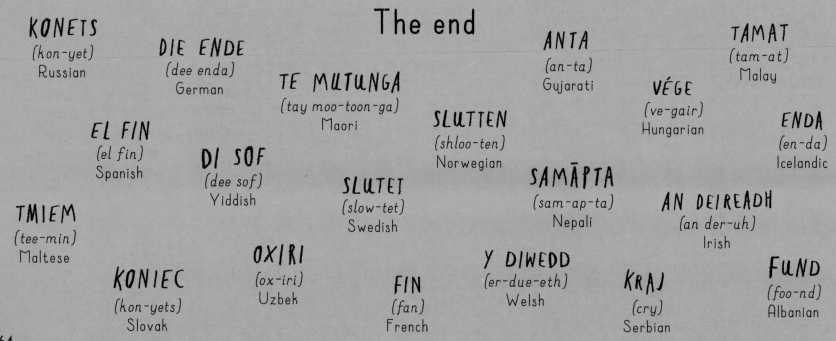

The end

KONETS
(kon-yet)
Russian

DIE ENDE
(dee enda)
German

TE MUTUNGA
(tay moo-toon-ga)
Maori

EL FIN
(el fin)
Spanish

DI SOF
(dee sof)
Yiddish

SLUTTEN
(shloo-ten)
Norwegian

SLUTET
(slow-tet)
Swedish

ANTA
(an-ta)
Gujarati

VÉGE
(ve-gair)
Hungarian

SAMĀPTA
(sam-ap-ta)
Nepali

TAMAT
(tam-at)
Malay

ENDA
(en-da)
Icelandic

AN DEIREADH
(an der-uh)
Irish

TMIEM
(tee-min)
Maltese

KONIEC
(kon-yets)
Slovak

OXIRI
(ox-iri)
Uzbek

FIN
(fan)
French

Y DIWEDD
(er-due-eth)
Welsh

KRAJ
(cry)
Serbian

FUND
(foo-nd)
Albanian